Pocket ✂ ACTIVITY FUN and GAMES

HALLOWEEN

It's time for ghosts, ghouls, witches, and wizards to come out to play.

This book is filled with tricks and treats for Halloween and beyond—things to draw, puzzles, and spooky stickers!

BARRON'S

This Halloween book belongs to

....

WHAT'S INSIDE THIS BOOK?

THIS BOOK IS FRIGHTFULLY FUN!

Your Halloween book is packed with surprises and things that go bump in the night. You can write, draw, color, and fill up pages by being as spooky as you like.

MONSTER MAKE AND BAKE

Dress for the party with hats and costumes. Make monster feet and hang a skeleton. There is artistic paper to get creative with, too! And don't keep your party guests howling with hunger. Find recipes for pumpkin soup and vampire bites.

SPINE-CHILLING STICKERS

There are loads of cool stickers waiting for you in this book, along with foldout spine-chilling scenes. You can use your stickers here and with many more activities, including the creepy costume designs and the wizened wizard.

PUZZLES AND GAMES

With picture puzzles, spot-the-difference puzzles, and memory games, there's plenty to keep a ghost from his grave.

First edition for North America published in 2014 by Barron's Educational Series, Inc.

This is a Carlton book
Text, design, and illustrations
copyright © Carlton Books 2014

Author: William Potter
Illustrations: Chris Gould and Anna Stiles

Published in 2014 by Carlton Books Limited,
an imprint of Carlton Publishing Group,
20 Mortimer Street, London, W1T 3JW

All inquiries should be addressed to Barron's Educational Series, Inc.
250 Wireless Boulevard
Hauppauge, NY 11788
www.barronseduc.com

ISBN 978-1-4380-0516-4

Date of Manufacture: May 2014
Manufactured by Leo Marketing, China.

Printed in Heshan, China

9 8 7 6 5 4 3 2 1

Product conforms to all applicable CFSC and CPSIA 2008 standards. No lead or phthalate hazard.

PICTURE CREDITS

The publishers would like to thank the following sources for their kind permission to reproduce the pictures in this book.

Key: T: Top, B: bottom, L: Left, R: Right, C: Center

Stock XCHNG: 4, 5, 18, 19 (frames), 5, 15 (background) 48tr, 49tr, 48b, 49b, 62, 63 (background)
iStockphoto.co.uk: 10, 40, 41, 57 (scroll)
Thinkstockphotos.co.uk: 11, 12, 30, 31 (background), 48c, 49c, 48r

Every effort has been made to acknowledge correctly and contact the source and/or copyright holder of each picture and Carlton Books Limited apologizes for any unintentional errors or omissions, which will be corrected in future editions of this book

PREPARE TO SCARE!

WARNING! Only witches, wizards, vampires, ghosts, or zombies are allowed past this point!

Take the Terrible Test below to proceed further.

○ Do you like to stay up late?

○ Do you like to bite people?

○ Do your raggedy clothes stink?

○ Do you like to creep up on people?

○ Do you wish you could turn people into frogs?

○ Do you hate cleaning your room?

○ Do you have hairy hands and feet?

If you checked off one or more of the boxes, this book is for you.

Now turn the page, if you dare!

SPOOKY SNAPS

Meet the monsters and ghouls that come out on Halloween night. Who would you most like to meet in a dark and misty cemetery?

Draw your face on your favorite critter, and your friends' and family's faces on the others.

GHOST

LONG AGO, THIS GHOST WAS A QUIET OLD LADY WHO LIVED IN YOUR NEIGHBORHOOD. THEN SHE HAD A TERRIBLE ACCIDENT AND SHE COMES BACK YEAR AFTER YEAR TO WAIL AND MOAN ABOUT IT.

WITCH

THIS WITCH LOOKS PRETTY BUT THAT'S ONLY BECAUSE SHE'S CAST A SPECIAL BEAUTY SPELL ON HERSELF. AVOID DRINKING HER POTIONS. YOU WON'T LOOK GOOD AS A WARTY TOAD OR A HAIRY SPIDER!

VAMPIRE

THE COUNT WANTS TO GET CLOSE SO HE CAN
BITE YOU ON THE NECK AND SLURP YOUR BLOOD.
IF YOU LET HIM, YOU'LL BECOME A VAMPIRE, TOO
AND HAVE TO SPEND ALL DAY IN A COFFIN AND
TURN INTO A BAT AT NIGHT. SOUNDS LIKE FUN!

HOW TO DRAW A SCARY FACE

Copy each step to draw your own scary face on the bottom right. You can use it to decorate Halloween cards or party invites.

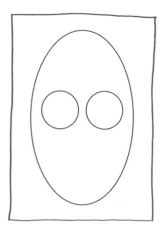

1. Draw an oval with two large, round eyeholes.

2. Sketch two slits for the nostrils and a wide, open mouth.

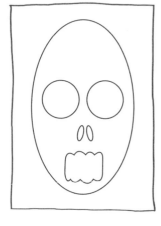

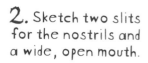

3. Add teeth in the mouth, a crack on the head, and two curves on either side of the eyes.

4. Finish with a fright by drawing a pair of googly eyes and fill in the smile and eyeholes with black.

FRIGHTFUL
FACT

TWO THOUSAND YEARS AGO IN MONGOLIA, IT WAS THE TRADITION FOR BARBARIAN WARRIORS TO USE THE SKULLS OF THEIR SLAIN ENEMIES AS DRINKING CUPS.

KOOKY CLOAKROOM

Time to choose your ideal Halloween costume.

Take a look at the clothes hanging in the closets and stored on the shelves. Then, design an outfit to scare the neighborhood.

You can use your stickers, too!

AMAZING
THINGS TO DO WITH YOUR
PARTY PAPER

1. Draw shapes on the back of the paper (there's more paper on pages 25–28). Then cut them out to use as book and binder decorations. Or, add them to a sheet of black paper and stick it on the wall for a monstrous mural.

2. Fold one of the designs in half to make a haunting Halloween greeting card or party invite. Stick your own bloodcurdling drawing on the front.

3. Use the patterns to make LABELS for your magic potions, or to cover your book of magic spells.

4. You could even cover a book of secrets and warn people to KEEP OUT!

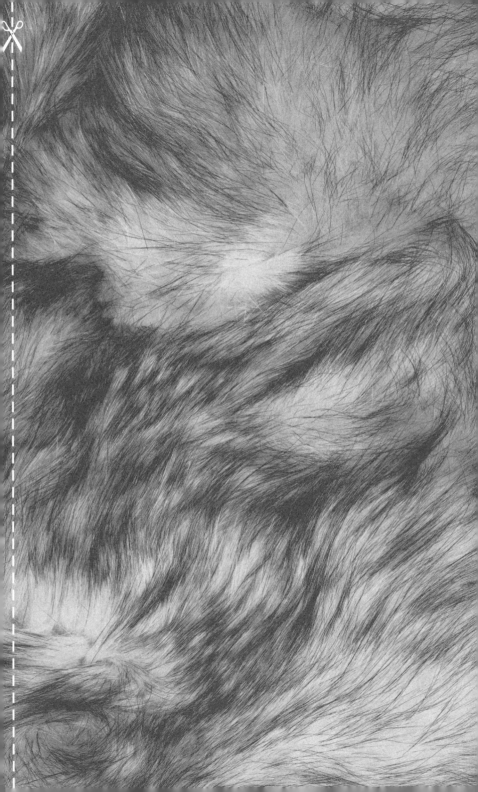

WITCH STYLE

Wynona the Witch is going to a Halloween party!

Use the color code below to help her glam up her outfit for the big night.

1 🦇 Black
2 🦇 Green
3 🦇 Skin color
4 🦇 Purple
5 🦇 Pink
6 🦇 Yellow
7 🦇 Brown

BATS ABOUT

Vampire bats are flitting through the moonlight in search of blood.

Look carefully at the silhouettes of the bats.

Can you find **10 pairs** and one extra?

The bat left over is the one that wants to bite you!

The answer is on page 96.

FRIGHTFUL FACTS

VAMPIRE BATS LIVE IN CENTRAL AND SOUTH AMERICA. THEY FEED AT NIGHT, BITING A HOLE IN THE FLESH OF SLEEPING ANIMALS BEFORE LAPPING UP THEIR BLOOD. Slurp!

MAGIC POTIONS

Here's some frightful, fruity juice to share with your wizard and witch pals next time they come over for a spell.

GREEN GOO

INGREDIENTS:
Lime-flavored syrup
Apple juice
Lemonade
Handful of green grapes, cut into halves
Gummy worm candy

Pour ½" of lime syrup into a tall glass, then add apple juice until it is half-full.

Top it off with lemonade and sprinkle grape halves on top. Drape a gummy worm over the side of the glass.

SPOOKY SNAPS

Meet the monsters and ghouls that come out on Halloween night. Who would you most like to meet in a dark and misty cemetery?

Draw your face on your favorite critter, and your friends' and family's faces on the others.

ZOMBIE
LIKE THE MUMMY, THIS ZOMBIE WAS SNUG AS A BUG IN HIS GRAVE, WHERE HE WAS SLOWLY ROTTING, UNTIL MAGIC BROUGHT HIM BACK TO LIFE.

FRANKENSTEIN'S MONSTER
DR. FRANKENSTEIN MADE THIS MONSTER FROM A COLLECTION OF DEAD BODY PARTS. THEY DIDN'T FIT TOGETHER WELL, SO THE MONSTER'S NOT VERY HAPPY AND CAN'T FIND ANY CLOTHES TO FIT HIM.

WEREWOLF

AT FULL MOON, THIS POOR GUY GETS FURRY AS HE BECOMES HALF MAN, HALF WOLF. LISTEN CAREFULLY AND YOU'LL HEAR HIM HOWLING OUTSIDE—TOO CLOSE FOR COMFORT!

MUMMY

ONCE HE WAS AN EGYPTIAN PRINCE. WHEN HE DIED HE WAS WRAPPED UP AND BURIED IN A TOMB. FIVE THOUSAND YEARS LATER, SOMEONE WOKE HIM UP AND WE WERE ALL CURSED!

19

MONSTERS ON THE LOOSE!

THEY'VE ESCAPED! Design your own monsters and show them breaking free from their cages.

You could give them
tentacles, claws, fangs,
hair, horns, or spikes—
go craaaaaazy!

WITCH'S AND WIZARD'S WARDROBE

Do you need help with a super-spooky outfit for Halloween?
Here are some excellent eerie ideas!

MAKE A WITCH'S OR WIZARD'S HAT

You will need

Black construction paper 💀 String ⚙ ruler ❀ scissors
Pushpin 🕷 pencil 🕷 stapler 👻 glue
Paint and paintbrush 🕷 Your stickers

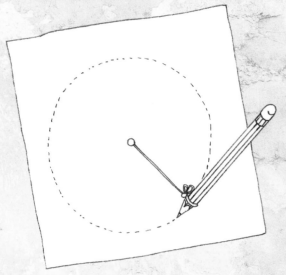

1. Cut a 9" length of string and tie one end to a pencil. Pin the other end to the center of your paper, to mark out a large circle about 16" in diameter as shown. Draw another circle in the same way, and cut both out.

⚡ CAREFUL! ⚡

Ask a grown-up for help when using anything sharp.

2. Fold one circle and cut it in half. Roll this semicircle to make a cone with a hole that's the right fit for your head. Ask a grown-up to staple the bottom seam together. Then glue the edges together and leave it to dry.

3. Draw around the bottom of the cone in the center of the other circle and cut this out to shape the brim. Cut slits in the base of the cone to make flaps. Fold these over so you can glue them to the underside of the brim.

4. When the glue is dry, decorate your magic hat with spooky drawings and stickers. You could also use paint or glitter glue.

HAIRY HORROR

There's a full moon!

Turn poor Johnny Lupus into a werewolf by drawing on wolf ears, claws, frightening fangs, and lots of shaggy hair all over his body.

FRIGHTFUL FACTS

HUNGARIAN LEGENDS TELL THAT WEREWOLVES LIVED IN AN AREA CALLED TRANSDANUBIA. CHILDREN WHO RAN AWAY BECAME ABLE TO CHANGE INTO WEREWOLVES THAT HUNTED AND FED ON WILD ANIMALS AT NIGHT.

MONSTER MIRTH

Fill in the word balloons to make some hilarious
Halloween jokes, then cackle like a crazy witch!

MAGIC MIRRORS

Suraman the Wizard
has two magic
mirrors.
They don't always
reflect the same
things!

Can you spot **10** differences
between the two reflections?

The answer is on page 96.

OUT-OF-SIGHT FRIGHT

Screaming Scarlett is running from an invisible monster. She can hear it howling! Connect-the-dots to reveal the hidden ghoul.

The answer is on page 96.

SLURPY SOUP

Pumpkins are not just for carving.

Here's a recipe for a delicious pumpkin soup that you can serve using the pumpkin as the bowl!

BE CAREFUL!
Ask a grown-up for help with the chopping, cooking, and serving in this recipe!

INGREDIENTS

Medium pumpkin ✦ 1 onion, peeled ◉ 1 tablespoon olive oil
2 teaspoons cumin powder ◎ 4 cups warm vegetable stock
1 tablespoon unflavored yogurt

STEPS

1. Cut away the top of the pumpkin. Scoop out the seeds and stringy bits inside.

2. Using a spoon, dig out the pumpkin flesh, being careful not to break through the sides of the pumpkin.

3. Chop the onion and fry it in the oil in a large pan for about five minutes.

4. Stir in the cumin, then add the chopped pumpkin flesh and stir it with the onions for about 10 minutes.

5. Pour in the warm stock and leave to simmer for 15 minutes until the pumpkin is soft.

6. Let the mixture cool a little before asking a grown-up to help you blend it into a soup. Pour the soup into the pumpkin shell and serve it to your Halloween guests with a ladle. Add a swirl of yogurt to each bowl.

MONSTER MASH

Igor has collected these body parts from the graveyard!

Copy them to build your own Frankenstein's monster, then bring him to life with color. And don't forget to add some sinister stitches and bolts to hold him together!

CREEPY COSTUMES

Make a dramatic entrance this Halloween
by swooping in as a vampire.

YOU WILL NEED

White shirt, black pants, and black shoes for a boy

Long, black dress and black boots for a girl

Long length of black fabric for a cape

Styling gel

Fake fangs

White and black face makeup

Fake blood

CREEPY COSTUMES

1. Put on your white shirt, pants, or dress.

3. FOR A BOY, push back and flatten your hair with styling gel, and use white makeup to cover your face. Add a point of black in the middle of your hairline and rings around your eyes.

FOR A GIRL, cover your face in white face paint, add black eyeliner, and paint your lips bright red.

2. Drape the cape over your shoulders and pin or tie it together at the neck.

Boys could also wear a bow tie and white gloves for more effect. And why not hang a toy bat inside your cape as a shocking surprise for your friends?

4. Put in your fangs and add drips of fake blood pouring from your lips.

MUMMIES UNWRAPPED

These mummies are coming undone.

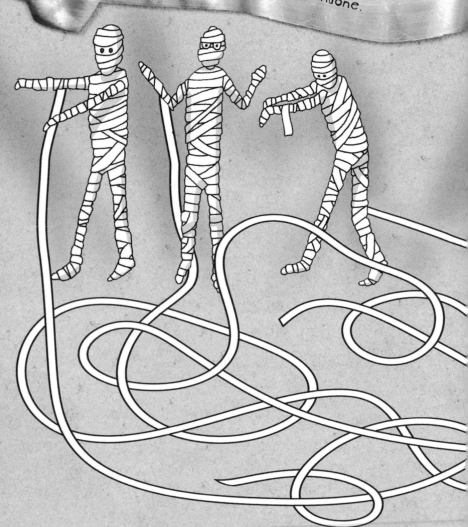

FRIGHTFUL FACTS

DURING THE PREPARATION OF A MUMMY, THE
DEAD PHARAOH'S BRAIN WOULD BE SCOOPED OUT
THROUGH HIS NOSTRILS USING A LONG HOOK!
THE PIECES OF BRAIN WERE THROWN AWAY AND
REPLACED WITH SAWDUST OR LINEN.

Follow the tangled bandages to find out which mummy got his bandages trapped under the lid of the sarcophagus.

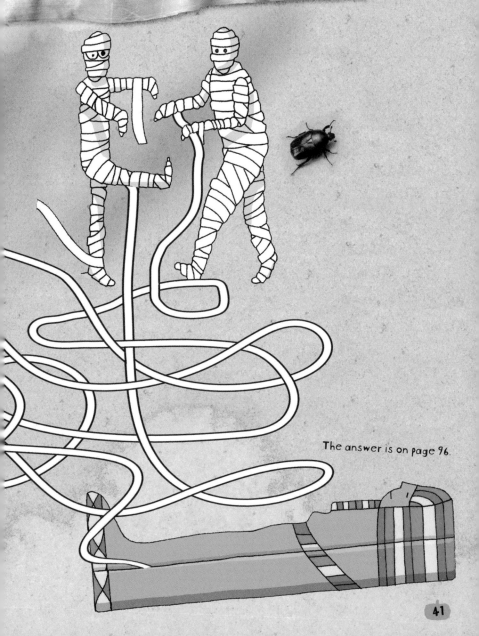

The answer is on page 96.

PERFECT PUMPKINS

Here's how to design the perfect jack-o'-lantern.

Draw these pictures onto your hollowed-out pumpkin, then ask a grown-up to carefully cut out the shapes. Put a candle inside to light up the lantern's fearsome features.

Starry sky

Draw lots of stars on your pumpkin for a stellar surprise.

Fangs a lot!

Draw triangular eyes and a wide, fanged grin for a vampire visage.

Frightful Facts

ORIGINALLY, JACK-O'-LANTERN WAS THE NAME GIVEN TO A FLAMING SPIRIT THAT INHABITED SWAMPY MARSHLANDS. THE SPIRIT WOULD LEAD LOST TRAVELERS TO THEIR DOOM IN THE DEEP BOGS.

Funky face

Use crescent moons for eyebrows, small circles for the eyes, and draw a goofy, toothy smile.

Bloodcurdling bat

Copy a bat shape on both sides of your pumpkin.

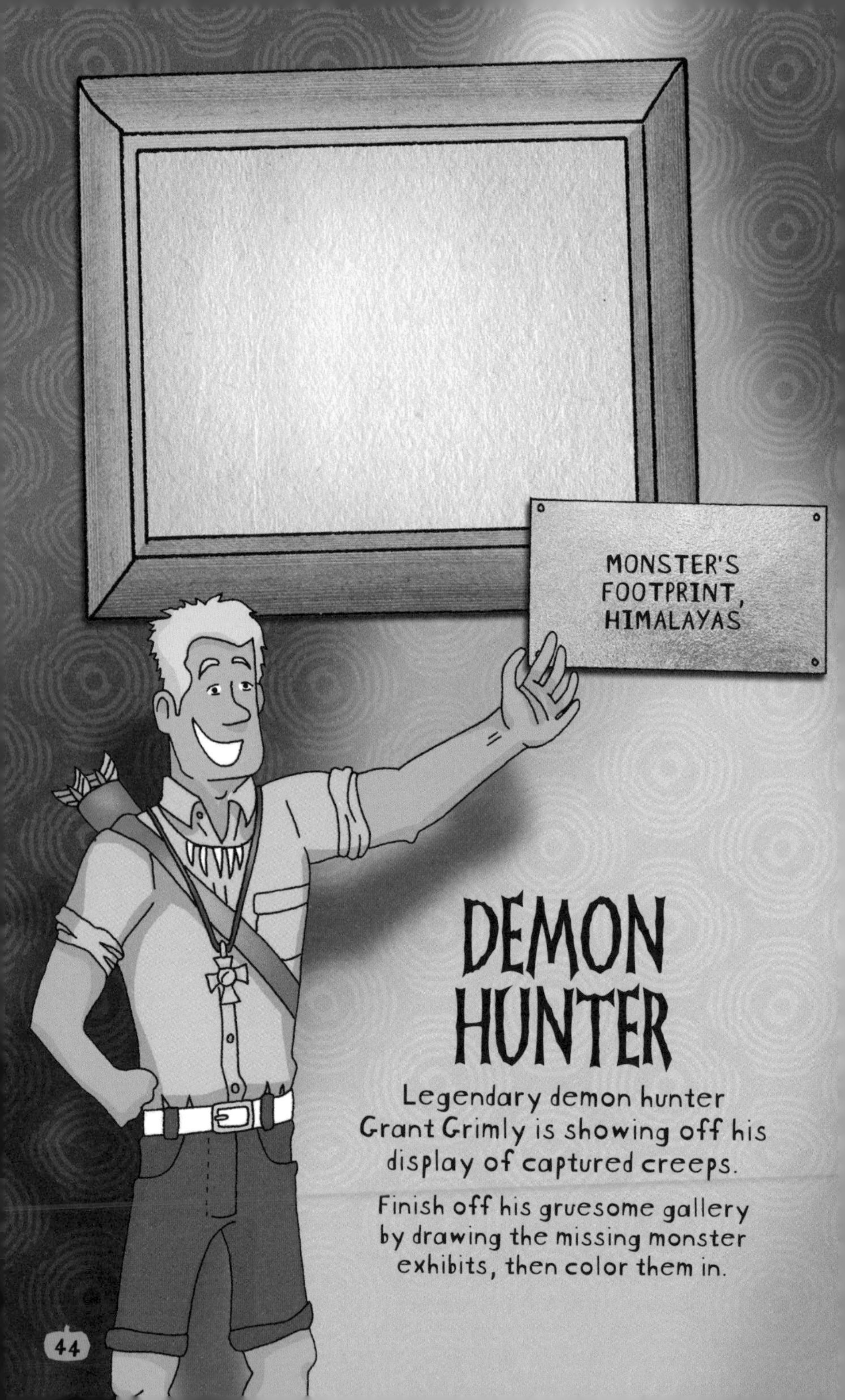

MONSTER'S
FOOTPRINT,
HIMALAYAS

DEMON HUNTER

Legendary demon hunter Grant Grimly is showing off his display of captured creeps.

Finish off his gruesome gallery by drawing the missing monster exhibits, then color them in.

VAMPIRE,
TRANSYLVANIA

SEAWEED CREATURE FROM
LOCH HAGGIS, SCOTLAND

TALE OF TERROR

Make up your own ghost story.

There are blanks in this spine-chilling tale for you to add names, places, and your scariest ideas.

Once it's finished, go share it with a friend... late at night.

LATE ON HALLOWEEN NIGHT, a mist descended on _____. (Your name here) was soon lost and reached a dead end at an old iron gate. The gate was rusty and covered in _____, as if it had not been opened for centuries. Tired and hungry, (Your name here) pushed through and walked up to the house to ask for directions.

The house looked _____. (Your name here) glimpsed a _____ moving past an upstairs window and felt a chill.

There was a _____ sound from within and footsteps. (Your name here) stepped back and was grabbed by the ankle. It was a _____ reaching from the muddy ground. Then, the door opened and there stood _____ wearing _____. It spoke in a voice from beyond the grave and said "_____."

(Your name here) struggled to get free, but it was too late. The monster leaped forward and _____. That was the last that anyone ever heard of (Your name here).

 THE GRISLY END

BRILLIANT BATS

Invite a colony of bats to your Halloween party with this ghoulish garland.

1. Copy the bat designs several times onto black construction paper and cut them out. You could fold the paper to cut out several bats at once.

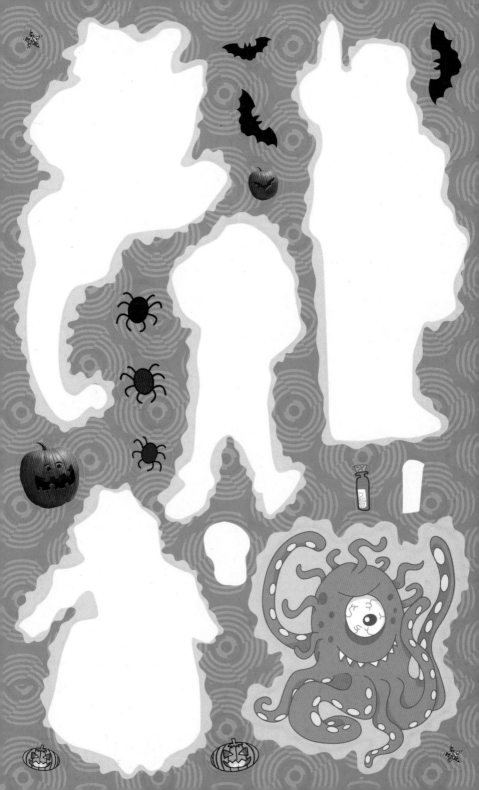

2. Carefully pierce holes for the eyes and on the wing tips, as marked. You could use a hole punch or push a pencil through the paper into modeling clay.

3. Thread your bats onto a length of string. Alternate the bats as you go along. Hang the garland in the party room.

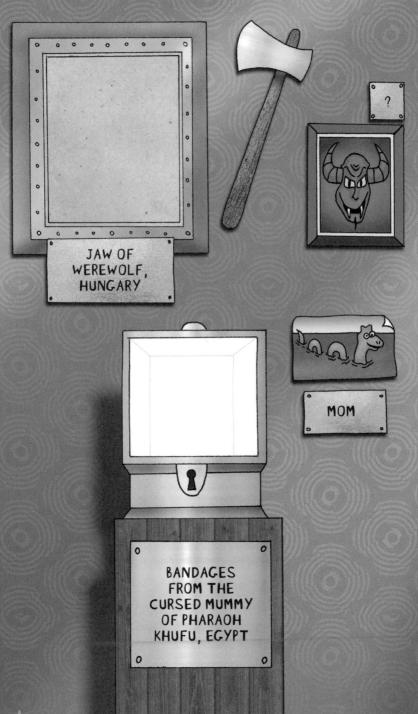

JAW OF
WEREWOLF,
HUNGARY

?

MOM

BANDAGES
FROM THE
CURSED MUMMY
OF PHARAOH
KHUFU, EGYPT

DEMON HUNTER

Garth Grimly is also a fearless demon hunter, just like his brother Grant. These are just some of the creepy things he's captured.

Finish off his gruesome gallery by drawing the missing exhibits, then color them in.

HORNED SKULL
—UNKNOWN CREATURE,
WISCONSIN, U.S.

GHOSTLY
ECTOPLASM,
MEXICO.
ONE HUNDRED PERCENT HAUNTED!

ZOMBIE'S ARM, HAITI

FREAKY FEET

Something weird is afoot! Here's how to make your own wacky werewolf feet to stomp around the neighborhood.

1. Draw around each side of one tissue box to measure out enough fur to cover both boxes. (If you don't have fake fur, you can paint your boxes with hairy monster patterns or scales.)

2. Make the claws. Cut out six foam or cardboard triangles with a flap at the base of each. Attach three claws to each box by gluing the flaps so that the claws stick out from the end. Glue the fur to the boxes. Make sure the claws stick out and leave the holes free for your feet.

3. Stuff the boxes with spare foam or newspaper, as padding for your feet. When the glue is dry you can put on your freaky feet and go out howling!

YOU WILL NEED:

Two empty tissue boxes big enough to fit on your feet

Brown or white fake fur, or paint and paintbrush

Glue, scissors, and green craft foam or cardboard

BODY SNATCHER

A ghoul has been creeping around the cemetery at night, digging up the fresh graves.

Don't let him steal everything!

Look at the contents of this open coffin and try to remember what's inside. Now turn the page and see if you can draw all **10** items!

Why not challenge a friend to see who can remember the most?

FRIGHTFUL FACTS
IN THE NINETEENTH CENTURY, RECENTLY BURIED BODIES WERE STOLEN FROM THEIR GRAVES AND SOLD TO MEDICAL SCHOOLS TO BE TAKEN APART FOR STUDY.

TERROR TEST

Now try to draw
all the things
you saw on
page 55.

KOOKY CLOAKROOM

Time to choose your ideal Halloween costume.

Take a look at the clothes hanging in the closets and stored on the shelves. Then, design an outfit to scare the neighborhood.

You can use your stickers, too!

FIND THE FORGERIES

This is Count Vincent Van Gore, the famous vampire artist. One of these pictures below is his self-portrait, but the other five are fakes!

A

B

C

D

E

F

Picture _____ is the REAL self-portrait.

The answer is on page 96.

WIZENED WIZARD

Old Wilfred the wizard has been using a potion to stay looking young, but he's run out of it!

Add wrinkles, bloodshot eyes, stubble, hairy ears, rotten teeth, and pimples to Wilfred to make him look hundreds of years old.

PETRIFYING POSTCARDS

Here's where you can write in
your monstrous messages:
Wish you were he-arrrrghhhhh!

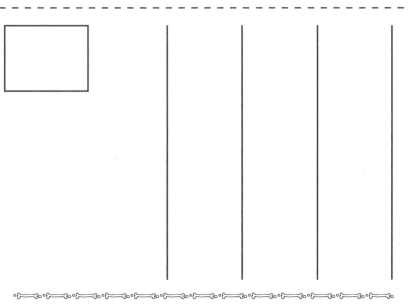

THE WITCH RETURNS

PETRIFYING POSTCARDS

Cut out and send gruesome greetings to friends and family with these cool postcards.

PETRIFYING POSTCARDS

Cut out and send gruesome greetings to friends and family with these cool postcards.

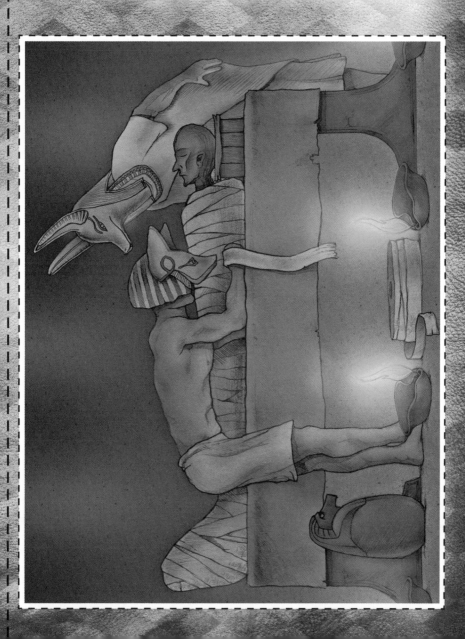

Here's where you can write in your monstrous messages:
wish you were he-arrrrghhhhh!

THE MUMMY

VAMPIRE BITES

Expecting a houseful of horrors?

These savory treats should keep them from feasting on you.

MUMMY'S FINGERS

INGREDIENTS:
Hot dogs, puff pastry, ketchup.

YOU WILL NEED:
Rolling pin, parchment paper, baking sheet.

1. Wrap thin strips of ready-made puff pastry around hot dogs to look like bandages.

2. Place them on parchment paper on a baking sheet.

3. Ask a grown-up to bake them in the oven for about 30 minutes, following the instructions on the pastry pack.

4. When they are cooked, cut them in half and add a dab of ketchup to the chopped end to look like blood.

UNINVITED GUESTS

Boy wizard Joey Maypole wanted to get in touch with his long-lost grandma, but he's reached a whole host of ghosts and demons as well.

Fill in the spaces using the stickers on your sticker sheets to find out who's come to say hi.

MORE VAMPIRE BITES

Expecting a houseful of horrors?

These savory and sweet treats should keep
them from feasting on you.

SKELETON COOKIES

INGREDIENTS:
Gingerbread cookie dough mix, white frosting.

YOU WILL NEED:
Rolling pin, gingerbread man cookie cutter,
parchment paper, baking sheet, decorating bag.

1. Roll out a sheet of cookie dough, about a quarter
of an inch thick.

2. Use the cookie cutter to
shape several figures.

3. Place them on parchment paper
on a baking sheet.

4. Ask a grown-up to bake them in the oven,
following the instructions on the cookie dough pack.

5. When the gingerbread men are baked, leave them
to cool.

6. Put the frosting into a decorating bag, then
decorate the cookies with skulls and bones to give
each gingerbread man a skeleton.

Witch's Hat Surprises

INGREDIENTS:
Small chocolate ice cream cones, chocolate frosted cookies, small candies, frosting.

YOU WILL NEED:
Decorating bag.

1. Fill a cone with small candies. Cover the open edge of the cone with frosting.

2. Carefully push the chocolate side of the cookie onto the frosted cone to make a brim and glue the two pieces together.

3. Turn the cone-and-cookie hat over so the cookie is on the bottom. Add more frosting around the cone's base to hold the parts together and make a ribbon or buckle pattern.

TROVE OF TREATS

It's been a successful night of trick-or-treating for this boy.

Look at his pile of candies. He has five of his favorites in front of him. Can you find three more of each candy in his pile of goodies?

The answer is on page 96.

FIENDISH FEATURES

Fill in the words and draw pictures to complete this ghostly newspaper.

PARANORMAL NEWS

WRITE HEADLINE

Confused ghost Gary Ghoulish has been haunting the wrong house for 100 years. Having scared away 78 families from write address ,

Gary realized his mistake when finish story .

WANTED:

BODIES. Any condition considered. Call Dr. Stinkenfried, Flugelstadt 067

BLOOD NEEDED. Will collect. Call Transylvania 987

Chart-topper fill in name

has stunned fans by confessing she changes into a werewolf at night. Her fans all thought she was a vampire. fill in name

says she intends to perform as a werewolf on her next tour. Her new single, fill in song title,

from the album *Howlin' from the Heart* is out now.

POP STAR ADMITS
"I AM A WEREWOLF"

CAT-ASTROPHE!

Can you help Winsome the Witch? Her beloved cat has swallowed a magic potion and made 15 duplicates appear.

Which is Winsome's cat?

Find the cat that matches this description:

MY CAT IS BLACK WITH ONE WHITE SPOT.

HE HAS A LONG TAIL WITH A FLUFFY END.

HE HAS ONE ROUNDED EAR.

HE HAS GREEN EYES AND A PINK TONGUE.

HE HAS SIX WHISKERS.

3

4

1

2

5

6

ANSWER:

The answer is on page 96.

Frightful Facts

IN FOLKLORE, WITCHES POSSESSED DEMONS IN THE FORM OF CATS, WHO WOULD RUN EVIL ERRANDS AND SPY FOR THEM. MANY PEOPLE REFUSED TO TALK NEAR A CAT, IN CASE A WITCH FOUND OUT THEIR SECRETS.

POWERFUL POTION

Hubble bubble, what icky ingredients will you choose for your magical medicine?

Draw some horrible ingredients for your mixture in the bottle.

Then add a name for your concoction on the label.

What magic spell does your potion power?

PETRIFYING POSTCARDS

Cut out and send gruesome greetings to friends
and family with these cool postcards.

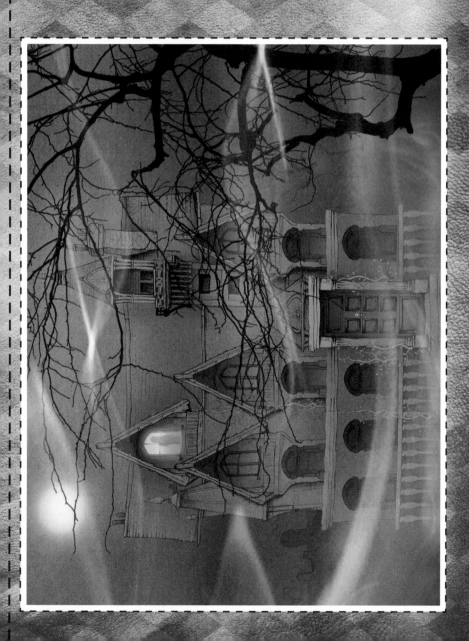

Here's where you can write in your monstrous messages:
Wish you were he-arrrrghhhhh!

THE HAUNTED HOUSE

HANGING BONES

Hang this dangling skeleton to spook any visitors.

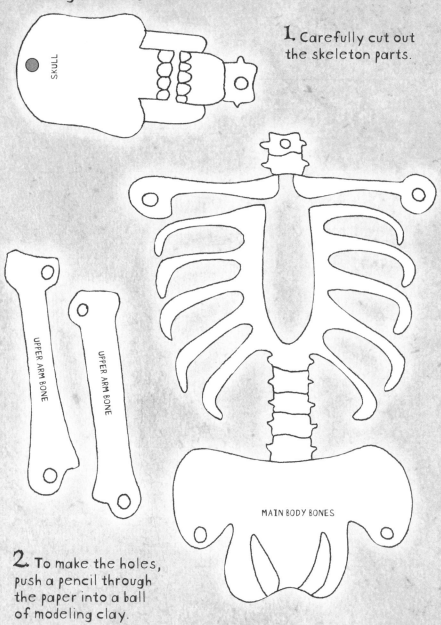

SKULL

1. Carefully cut out the skeleton parts.

UPPER ARM BONE

UPPER ARM BONE

MAIN BODY BONES

2. To make the holes, push a pencil through the paper into a ball of modeling clay.

3. Join the bones together with short lengths of yarn tied into small rings.

4. Use the hole in the skeleton's forehead to hang him from a piece of elastic, so his bones will bounce about.

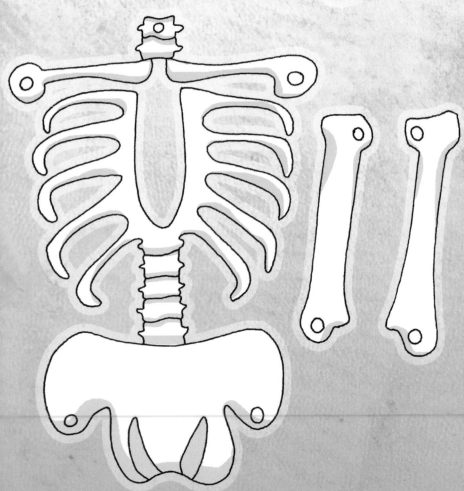

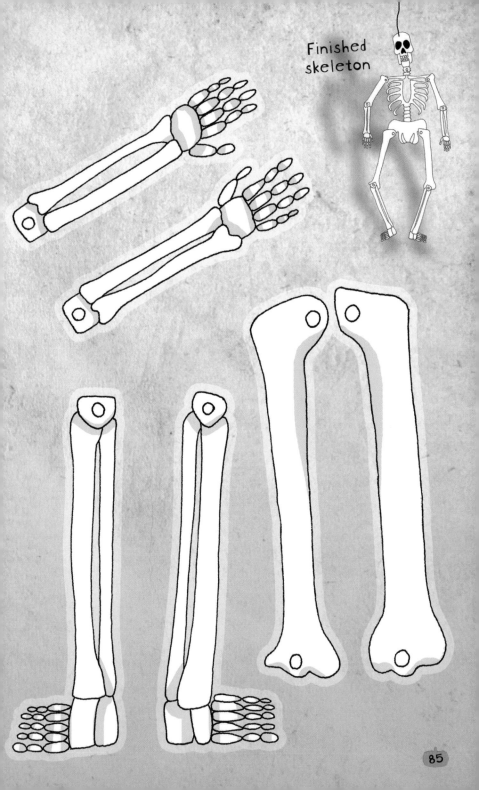

Finished
skeleton

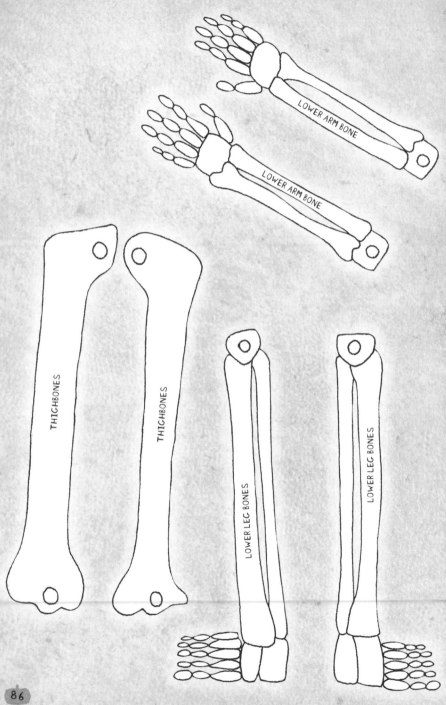

LOWER ARM BONE

LOWER ARM BONE

THIGHBONES

THIGHBONES

LOWER LEG BONES

LOWER LEG BONES

WHAT TO DO WITH YOUR SPOOKY STICKERS!

1. PLAY with your stickers over and over again on the fold out scary STICKER SCENES at the back of the book.

2. Make Halloween greeting cards from plain cardboard and DECORATE them with your stickers.

3. Use them to seal secret scrolls with magical wishes of good luck for your friends.

4. Stick them in places you think are haunted, as a WARNING.

FACELESS FIEND

Count Jackula looks sad.
Vampires don't have a reflection
so he can't check himself out
in the mirror.

Cheer him up by drawing his
face in the frame, with a
big, toothy smile.

FRIGHTFUL FACTS
ACCORDING TO LEGEND,
VAMPIRES HAVE NO REFLECTION
AND CAST NO SHADOW BECAUSE
THEY DON'T HAVE A SOUL.

SPOOK SPOTTER

Ghosts need friends, too.

Show how good a ghost spotter you
are by matching the ten pairs.
Draw lines between them.

The answers are on page 96.

PROFESSOR CRACKPOT

Fill in the spaces in the mad professor's lab of horrors using your stickers.

What monstrous creations has he come up with?

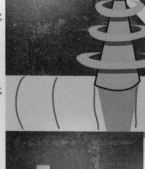

Get Ready to Party!

Here are some great game ideas for making your Halloween party a scream!

Zombie's Last Dinner

Put cold spaghetti (for intestines), sponges (brains), a tortilla (skin), corn silk (hair), and peeled grapes (eyeballs) in set Jell-O (cold flesh) in a large, covered bowl.

Then ask your friends to close their eyes and dip their hands into the "zombie's stomach" to find out what he had for his last dinner!

Apple Bobbing

Put two large buckets or bowls of water onto sheets of newspaper (to absorb splashes).

Drop about six apples into one bucket and ask your friends to put their hands behind their backs and try to move the apples from one bowl to the other using only their teeth. Vampires and werewolves are especially good at this!

Who can move the most apples in one minute?

CREEPY CONGRATULATIONS Well done! You've made it through Halloween alive! Here's your certificate. Sign and frame it in a place of pride.

CONGRATULATIONS!

You have passed the Halloween initiation tests with horrible honors

HAPPY SCARING!

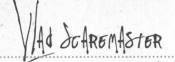

VLAD SCAREMASTER

Present this certificate at any branch of PETRIFYING PAM'S PESTILENT POTIONS STORE

for a 10% DISCOUNT on her range of essential magic ingredients.

ANSWERS